ASTROLOGY
AND
REINCARNATION

By

MANLY PALMER HALL

SECOND EDITION

MARTINO FINE BOOKS
Eastford, CT
2022

Martino Fine Books
P.O. Box 913,
Eastford, CT 06242 USA

ISBN 978-1-68422-718-1

Copyright 2022

Martino Fine Books

Cover Design Tiziana Matarazzo

Printed in the United States of America On 100% Acid-Free Paper

ASTROLOGY
AND
REINCARNATION

By

MANLY PALMER HALL

SECOND EDITION

PHILOSOPHICAL RESEARCH SOCIETY
1942

CONTENTS

———

NOTE—This text first appeared as articles in *Wynn's Astrology Magazine* and is reprinted with permission.

HOW TO READ YOUR PAST
AND FUTURE LIVES

THE science of Astrology had its beginning
with the most learned nations of antiquity.
The first astrologers, priests and philosophers,
found no conflict between the principles of
Astrology and the sacred philosophical systems which, ancient historians agree, were
first revealed to humanity by the gods. Thus
Astrology not only conforms with those universal laws which were the foundations of
ancient wisdom, but is also perfectly com-
patible with ancient standards of morality and
ethics.

Unfortunately, the philosophy of Astrology
finds few exponents in this modern age. Men,
more interested in material fortune than the
metaphysical mysteries of the soul, have ig-
nored the profounder issues of the astral science. But Brahmin sages in rock-hewn tem-
ples, Chaldean Magi on their lofty ziggurats,
Egyptian priests in their stone observatories,

did not devote thousands of years to the perfection of Astrology merely out of curiosity concerning their mundane affairs. To all of these wise ones the mysteries of the heavens were a revelation of divine principles and divine will. The handwriting of stars on the wall of heaven was to them in the very language of the gods.

The nations most given to astrological research also accepted the doctrine of the rebirth of human souls. Since these two important teachings, Astrology and Reincarnation, developed side by side, and the believers in the one teaching were also the exponents of the other, it is evident that no point of conflict exists between the belief in rebirth and the science of the stars.

The Hermetic philosophers, the wisest of the Egyptians, possessed a profound knowledge of both of these mysteries; as did also Pythagoras, Plato and Aristotle, the noblest thinkers among the Greeks. The Druid priests of Britain and Gaul included both Reincarnation and Astrology among their secret teachings. These noble men, revered as among the wisest and most virtuous of mortals, could not have been party to ignorance or superstition. In these matters then, we should consider their opinions with all seriousness.

Among Oriental nations the science of Astrology and the doctrine of Rebirth are still included together in the philosophy of life. Old Hindu textbooks on Astrology, attributed to the saints and Rishis, contain hints and allusions to the method of determining past and future states of existence from a natal horoscope. Among the lamas of Tibet secret formulas, carefully guarded from the profane, are still used by astrologer-priests to determine the parts of the previous existence from the positions of the stars at the beginning of this life.

The problems which these Tibetan priests seek to solve are comprehended under three headings:

1. The place of the spiritual entity among the *nidanas* or the sequences of consequences which cause the physical incarnation of the soul.

2. The level or plane of consciousness in which the entity functioned prior to its present life, which contributes the moral force to the present existence.

3. Such details and circumstances of the previous existence as may account for the karma, or processes of retribution, which are at work in the present existence.

In addition to these, a horoscope may be erected for the moment of death by which the future state of the soul or entity is estimated.

Altogether, this part of Astrology is concerned with that larger theatre of action of of which the present life is but a fragment. To all philosophic peoples, man's present state is the result of previous life and action. To understand this, is to discover the cause of present conditions. Asiatic astrologers have practiced this part of the science for thousands of years, and their findings should be of interest to western students of Astrology.

The principle behind the Bhava Chakra (or Cycle of Transmigratory Existence) recorded on the ceiling of the Lamaist monastery at Sikkim is entirely astrological. The outer circle of the figure is divided into 12 parts which are termed the *nidanas* or the causes which move the soul to rebirth. These *nidanas* are the 12 Zodiacal signs, each one of which contains within it an impulse to action or, as the ancients termed it, a cause of contact.

The first *nidana,* under Aries, is called the *unconscious will.* It is represented by a blind man and signifies the soul passing from death to rebirth.

The second *nidana,* under Taurus, is called *conformation,* and is represented by a potter and his pots, signifying the soul shaping the materials of the mental and physical natures.

The third *nidana,* under Gemini, is called the *conscious will,* and is typified by the restlessness of the monkey, and signifies the rise of conscious experience in the soul.

The fourth *nidana,* under Cancer, called *self-consciousness,* is represented by a ship containing man, woman, and animals, and signifies the rise of the quality of individuality.

The fifth *nidana,* under Leo, is represented by an empty house and signifies the development of the *sensory perceptions.*

The sixth *nidana,* under Virgo, is a figure representing *marriage,* and signifies the focussing of the sense perceptions upon exterior objects.

The seventh *nidana,* under Libra, is represented by a figure with an arrow in its eye, and signifies the *illusions of pain and pleasure,* and their reaction upon the soul.

The eighth *nidana,* under Scorpio, is called *desire* and is involved in the experiences of gratification.

The ninth *nidana,* under Sagittarius, is termed *indulgence* and is represented by a man collecting fruit into a basket. It signifies attachment to worldly possessions.

The tenth *nidana,* under Capricorn, represents *maturity* and signifies the fullness of material existence brought to its highest philosophical level.

The eleventh *nidana,* under Aquarius, is compensation represented by the birth of a son. This signifies the paying of all debts to nature and final detachment therefrom.

The twelfth *nidana,* under Pisces, shows the dead body being carried to the grave. It signifies decay of all points of contact by which the life is held to the material state.

After the twelfth, the first begins again, and so on through all the cycles of existence. The *nidanas,* of course, represent the dominating consciousness or the place of the spiritual Self in the great cycle of progress. While our little life has its birth, growth, maturity and decay, so many hundreds of these lives form together a greater cycle involving a vast process of life moving through its several stages.

By the position of the Sun the *nidana* is determined and by the Ascendant the subdivision of the *nidana* is ascertained. Thus a person born with the Sun in Pisces is born to the experience of detachment, for he is bringing a cycle of experience to an end. A person born with the Sun in Scorpio is born under the eighth *nidana* and the soul purpose of his existence is to experience the consequences of greed, personality and possession.

The Ascendant of the horoscope represents a minor cycle of experience within a greater one. It qualifies and specializes the general significance. Thus, for example, the fifth *nidana,* or Leo, is an externalizing of the sensory power and generally manifests as ambition. If the Ascendant is in the third *nidana,* or Gemini, representing the effort to establish individual sufficiency, it qualifies the major factor and denotes that the ambitions will be of an intellectual or mental nature. By calculations based upon this arrangement, the primary purpose of the soul's incarnation is established. In application, it is generally found that this purpose more or less dominates the individual in whose horoscope it is indicated.

In the Tibetan monastery figure, the central part of the design, representing the world or, more exactly, the conditions of consciousness which together make up the world, is divided into six parts. In the painting these parts or panels are filled with elaborate designs setting forth the condition of souls in various levels or degrees of spiritual development.

The six compartments of the circle are divided into an upper and lower hemisphere of three compartments each The upper hemisphere represents the three nobler states of being which are denominated in degrees of excellence: (1) the world of the gods; (2) the world of the Titans or Heroes; (3) the world of men. Together these three parts depict the happy states of consciousness which are the reward of good Karma, that is, lives of noble thought and action.

The three compartments of the lower hemisphere of the circle depict the miseries resultant from bad Karma or destructive thought, emotion and action. The three compartments are named respectively: (1) the world of animals; (2) the world of ghosts; (3) and the world of hells or spheres of violent retribution.

In each of these six parts of the world is also depicted a form of the Buddha symbolical of universal enlightenment, which regenerates and preserves evolving souls in all the spheres of being.

The Sun of course represents the Buddha, the power of difussed illumination. The solar energy, distributed through the natural creation, is the universal source of the impulse towards light and truth.

The six compartments through which the Sun's light shines pertain to the other major bodies of the solar system known to the old astrologers. The world of the gods is the sphere of Jupiterian consciousness; that of the Titans, Martial consciousness; that of human beings, Mercurial consciousness. These planets therefore dominate the upper hemisphere of the sphere of consciousness. Venus represents animal consciousness; the Moon the imaginative consciousness, termed the world of ghosts; and Saturn the retribution consciousness or the Karmic hells.

In the East it is taught that each soul coming into material life enters from one of the six compartments of the Wheel of the Law. Astrologically, the rule for determining the origin of the soul's present life cycle is as follows:

Examine the horoscope and discover whether the Sun or the Moon is the stronger. Determine this from position, dignity, and aspect. Then observe in which decanate the more powerful luminary is placed. Find the ruler of this decanate according to ordinary astrological practice, and the ruler of the decanate shall signify the sphere of consciousness or *Loka* from which the soul came into birth. Next examine the position of the planet which is ruler of the decanate as to its dignity, position, aspect, etc. From this determine the quality of the previous life. If the ruler of the decanate enjoys dignity and high position, the same would be true of the previous life of the native. If it is afflicted, cadent, or ill placed, the previous state of the life was lowly or unfortunate.

A similar system is practiced by the Brahmins. They consider only four worlds, but the method of determining this important matter is identical in both systems.

In Astrology the sign ascending on the Eastern angle of the heavens at the moment of birth is the general significator of the present incarnation, and the entire horoscope is read from this Ascendant, and all the testimonies of the chart are blended with the fundamental keynote of this ascending sign. The Zodiacal sign upon the cusp of the 12th house may be termed the preceding sign to the Ascendant, and the Zodiacal sign upon the cusp of the 2nd house may be termed the succeeding sign from the Ascendant. As the Ascendant signifies the present state of the evolving soul, the cusp of the 12th house becomes the significator of the previous life to the present one, and the sign upon the cusp of the 2nd house the next incarnation after the present one.

The rule is that angular houses signify the present life, succeedent houses the next life to come, and cadent houses the previous life and its Karma.

If then we move the horoscope sufficiently to bring the 12th house cusp to the Ascendant, we can then read the horoscope as the nativity of the previous life. Ordinarily the 12th house of the horoscope is termed the house of self-undoing, in that it reveals the fundamental weakness of character which undermine the probability of present success. The term "self-undoing" is identical in meaning with Karma, or the accumulations of past actions which overshadow present conditions. This accumulation is carried forward from life to life until all weaknesses are overcome and final perfection is achieved.

It naturally follows that whatever Zodiacal sign dominates the present life of the individual, the sign previous to it signifies the Karma brought forward from the past. The position of the ruler of that sign and planets in the 12th house reveal the circumstances of the previous existence, the probable place and time of the previous birth, and the general circumstances of that existence.

The sign Aries ascending indicates Pisces to have dominated the previous existence. Aries as the first sign of the Zodiac is the beginning of a new cycle of experience. Aries people have come into this life from a previous existence of limitation, responsibility and bondage. Their present life is therefore a release and they move forward, dominated by strong ambition and enthusiasm.

If Taurus is ascending they have brought forward the impulse of the previous Arian existence. Most Taurus people bring forward the positive militant attitudes of Aries and beneath their artistic surface emotional fires bear witness to the militancy of their previous incarnation.

When Gemini ascends we find beneath the intellectual attitude the Karmic pressure of Taurus. The superficiality of the Gemini temperament is evident throughout this country, which is strongly Mercurial. Yet under the general intellectual surface of the nation is a powerful and despotic, economic force that is a distinct Taurian hangover.

When Cancer ascends, Gemini lurks in the background. Cancer people are subject to the distorted imaginations of a negative and uncontrolled Mercury. It is hard for Cancer people to be natural and relaxed, for behind them is a life lived under the influence of a negative Mercury agitating the intellect by a complex of opinions and fears that are too often allowed to grow into facts.

When Leo is ascending there is generally a strength complex arising out of the weakness of the previous life. For this reason Leo people are apt to be egotistic and power-loving, building a positive outward front to protect a very sensitive, emotional, imaginative, subjective nature held over from the Cancer influence.

When Virgo is ascending there is a subconscious repentance in the soul. The previous life was under the forceful, dominating influence of Leo. The Leo incarnation revealed the emptiness and vainness of authority and the native is born into Virgo with a strong tendency to the simple life. Virgo is a sign of atonement and the individual has the impulse to help a world which he probably tyrannized over in the previous life. Down deep inside of themselves many people have rather a definite Leo superiority complex and a tendency to boss.

When Libra ascends the individual brings into life Virgo karma. The people of Virgo have a tendency to lean and depend, and this weakness comes forward in Libra as a sense of internal insufficiency. The Libra native is of an artistic, somewhat irritable, delicate temperament. They have strong vanity arising out of their Virgo repentance.

When Scorpio ascends, the strong emotional power of the previous life combines its force with the fiery nature of this sign. Libra is artistic and emotional with a tendency to melancholy. Scorpio intensifies these qualities, giving also depth and organization to the thought. The self-gratification of Libra is the natural foundation for the powerful ambitions of Scorpio.

The sign Sagittarius ascending produces a jovial temperament, but the Scorpio qualities of the previous life are also present here, producing their love of the mysterious, religious and philosophic aspirations, a strong emotional nature, a love of power and position, and danger of over indulgence. The schemes and plots of Scorpio are released as vast promotion projects by the Sagittarians.

It may at first seem improbable that we should find much of Sagittarius in the Capricornian. With Capricorn rising, however, we find great emphasis upon the ambitions and a considerable measure of the Sagittarian concept of justice. When Capricorn ascends the individual generally feels that he is limited or inhibited. The large Jupiterian promotions of his previous life are curtailed by the Saturnine limitations of his present sphere of action, so he is dissatisfied and repressed.

As Capricorn is the most limited sign in the zodiac (a limitation, however, mostly self-imposed) it is natural that the next incarnation should be a revolt against limitation. The result is the Aquarian whose life is often dedicated to unconventionality. With Aquarius rising, there is a general revolt against precedent, convention, and conservativeness. Generous in large matters, Aquarians often retain a selfishness in small things essentially Capricornian.

Pisces is the last sign of the Zodiac and this sign brings to an end the cycle of Karma set in motion in Aries. People with this sign rising will therefore usually have rather hectic lives, gathering up the loose ends of unfinished business. From Aquarius, the preceding sign, comes vacillation, inconsistency, and nervousness. From all the preceeding signs come responsibilities and problems to be assimilated and transmuted into soul power. It is the particular duty of the Piscean to put his life in order and prepare himself for a new beginning and a higher level of action. Pisces is the weakest of the signs because it represents the end of a cycle of experience.

By reading the 12th house as the Ascendant, the general pattern of the previous life can be determined with reasonable detail and we can discover the subtle forces which have brought us up to our present state and dominate our present life in this world. Through the understanding of this branch of Astrology we can appreciate the old philosophical belief that all that we are today is the result of what we have been, and that what we will be tomorrow must be the result of what we are today. We learn from the past, we labor in the present, and we build for the future.

ASTROLOGY AND REINCARNATION

FLAVIUS Claudius Julian, generally known as the Apostate Emperor of Rome, was born at Constantinople November 6, A. D. 331. He propitiated the god Mercury as Lord of his geniture, and from this circumstance, checked by his appearance and the circumstances of his life, it appears that he was born with the sign of Gemini ascending.

Julian was by far the most learned and philosophical of the Roman emperors and probably also exceeded all the others in personal virtue and integrity. At the time of his birth the Flavian family, rulers of Rome, was nominally Christian as the result of the conversion of Constantine, surnamed the Great. Julian was educated as a Christian in Nicomedia by the Bishop Eusebius and even officiated as a lecturer in the Christian church.

The circumstances which caused Julian to denounce the Christian faith and return to the pagan doctrines of the classical world have been variously described. The young man was of an extremely religious and sensitive

(19)

nature, with strong development of the faculty of veneration. His fine sense of values led him early to the realization of the greatness of Pythagoras, Plato and Aristotle. His childhood brought him in constant contact with the iniquities of the Christian house of Flavian. The Christian emperor Constantius massacred Julian's father and most of his relatives, banished his half brother Gallus to Ionia, and spared Julian only because of his extreme youth. A third factor in Julian's conversion to paganism was probably the Grecian influence in the prevailing educational system. Julian's teachers were men who highly venerated the Grecian philosophies and early instilled the old lore into the young man's mind.

In his twentieth year Julian was secretly initiated into the Mysteries of the Ephesians by the priest-philosopher Maximus, and four years later in Athens he was solemnly accepted into the Mysteries of Eleusus. He may therefore be regarded as one of the last great initiates of the pagan world.

There is no evidence that Julian ever persecuted the Christians, although he wrote a powerful essay against the corruptions of their faith. It is certain, however, that he gave favor in government to pagans, and surrounded himself with philosophers and priests of non-Christian rites.

The call to the purple came on his birthday, November 6, A. D. 355, which seems to check the probability of the accuracy of his horoscope as given. The responsibilities of government weighed heavily upon the soul of the philosopher-emperor and interfered seriously with the development of his religious ideals. But it has been said of him that he penetrated as far in philosophy as the responsibilities of empire would permit.

Representations of the Emperor Julian portray him as a man of noble visage, heavy beard, prominent nose, and a definitely Scorpio asymmetry of features. He described himself as being utterly indifferent to the formalities of rulership and the niceties of personal appearance. He tells us that even while campaigning he continued his studies and writing, and that on the battlefield his fingers were stained with ink. Bound by the circumstances of the times in which he lived, Julian nevertheless represented a standard of personal integrity far above the majority of his contemporaries and worthy of recognition in any age.

The historian Libanius thus describes Julian's amazing life and temperament: "Always abstemious, and never oppressed by food, he applied himself to business with the activity of a bird, and dispatched it with infinite ease. In one and the same day he gave several audiences; he wrote to cities, to magistrates, to generals of armies, to his absent friends, to those who were on the spot; hearing letters read that were addressed to him, examining petitions, and dictating with such rapidity that the short-hand writers could not keep pace with him. He alone had the secret of hearing, speaking, and writing at the same time; and in this multitude of complicated operations he never mistook. After having dispatched business, and dined merely through urgent necessity, shutting himself up in his library, he read and composed till the instant when affairs of state summoned him to other labours. A supper still more sparing than the dinner was followed by a sleep as light as his meals. He awaked in order to labour with other secretaries whom he had allowed to sleep on the preceding day. His ministers were obliged to relieve each other; but, as for himself, he knew no repose but the change of employment. He alone was always labouring, he multiplied himself, and assumed as many forms as Proteus. Julian was pontif, author, diviner, judge, general of the army, and, in all these characters, the father of his country."

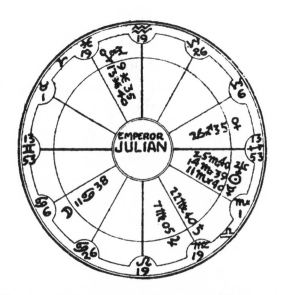

Flavius Claudius Julian, Emperor
of Rome, born Nov. 6, 331 A. D.,
6:20 P. M.

The extraordinary personality of Julian is well shown in his horoscope. There is a grand trine of planets in the watery triplicity, abundantly testifying to the accounts of various historians who describe his devotion to the mystical and occult arts. It is seldom that one discovers a nativity containing a grand trine involving the Sun, the Moon, the ruler of the chart and the Lord of the Mid-heaven.

Thomas Taylor, the eminent Platonist, in his *Introduction to the Orations of the Emperor Julian,* observes: "The grandeur of his soul is so visible in his composition, that we may safely credit what he asserted of himself, that he was formerly Alexander the Great, and if we consider the actions of Alexander and Julian, we shall easily be induced to believe that it was one and the same person."

If it is possible to discover from the positions of the planets any key to the previous life of an individual, no better example could be chosen for study than the horoscope of the initiate Julian. By virtue of his acceptance into the sacred body of pagan learning, he should be particularly qualified to pass judgment concerning the condition of his previous existence. As a pagan, Julian was well informed concerning the action of the law of rebirth.

Let us now turn for a moment to the life of Alexander the Great. Unfortunately we are without a correct horoscope of his nativity. In 1662 the English astrologer John Gadbury published a horoscope purported to be that of Alexander, but the 17th century was notoriously inaccurate in matters regarding history, and as early as 1697 the astrologer Partridge exposed the improbability in the accepted birth date of Alexander. Modern historians have shown the old nativity to be incorrect not only in month and day, but in the year also. According to Hogath, probably the most reliable authority on the subject, Alexander the Great was born B. C. 356, probably in the month of October. Portraitures of Alexander and written descriptions of his appearance agree in general that he was a man of medium height, of strong, squarely built body. The head was large, the face somewhat flat, the eyes large and wide apart, the forehead low with a heavy prominent lock or tuft of hair low in the center. His eyes are described as liquid and melting. The neck was somewhat large, the chin square, and the lips full. In other words, we have a pretty good description of a Taurean, nor is there lack of precedent of the conquering power of Taurus ascending. George Washington had this sign rising, and it dominated the nativity of General Grant. From Hogath's data, the Sun sign was most likely Libra. This sign is also often associated with leadership and conquering genius. According to the given time, Napoleon I had Libra rising, and another example of the ambitions of this sign is Adolph Hitler. Gandhi also has the Sun in Libra.

The lives of Alexander and Julian certainly parallel in many respects. Both men were devoted to classical learning. Alexander the Great respected his tutor Aristotle above all other men. On one occasion he declared Aristotle to be far dearer to him than his own father, for he said, "My father gave me being, but Aristotle gives me well-being." The youth of both Alexander and Julian was similarly involved in conspiracies and disasters. Both men died at an early age. There was only one year's difference in the length of their lives. Alexander died of poison, Julian of a wound. Both died at a distance from their native lands, while on campaigns of conquest, and the places of death were not far removed. Alexander died in Babylon, Julian in Assyria.

Following the rules set forth in the preceding chapter, let us examine the chart of Julian. The first rule is to observe which of the luminaries is most dignified, and take the ruler of the decan as the significator of the estate and condition of the previous life. The Sun and Moon are both highly dignified in the chart of Julian, but the Moon enjoys the added strength of being in its own sign. The Moon is in the second decan of Cancer which is under the rulership of Scorpio, therefore Mars is the significant planet. From this we should read that in his previous incarnation Julian should have been a soldier or some person engaged in Martial pursuits. In Julian's nativity Mars is in the 10th house, the house of kingship, leadership and honors, and so placed in part of the grand trine enjoying powerful benefic aspects from the Sun, Moon, and Mercury. It would be perfectly proper according to the most conservative rules of Astrology to declare Mars so placed to represent an extraordinary measure of Martial dignity and a royal or at least highly honored position among men.

Our second rule relates to the progress of the Sun and Ascendant from life to life. According to this, the sign on the cusp of the 12th house should indicate the Ascendant of the previous life, and the sign previous to the Sun sign should represent the Sun sign of the previous life. If Alexander was born in October, it is quite reasonable to suppose that his Sun sign could have been Libra, which is the sign previous to the Sun sign of the Emperor Julian. The description of Alexander is so definitely Taurean that it is well within possibility that he had Taurus rising. Alexander believed himself to be the incarnation or embodiment of the god Dionysus. This divinity was frequently depicted with the horns of a bull, and is usually associated by mythologists with the sign of Taurus. It is therefore quite possible that Alexander propitiated Dionysus as the diety of his ascending hour in the same way that Julian propitiated Mercury.

Some astrologers maintain that the sign ruling the 12th house may indicate the nationality of the previous life. Taurus rules Greece. To follow out this theory, that the 12th house cusp signifies the previous incarnation, turn the chart of Julian so that the cusp of the 12th becomes the Ascendant, and discover if possible to what degree this position could represent the life of Alexander. To point out a few possibilities, Capricorn becomes the ruler of the Midheaven. Capricorn governs India, and it was one of Alexander's greatest ambitions to convert the Hindus to Grecian art and religion. Mars and Uranus are in the 11th house, to represent Alexander's hopes, ideals and ambitions. May not the grand trine focussing upon these planets signify the extreme emphasis of ambition in the life of Alexander, who wailed to his generals that there were no more worlds to conquer? Sagittarius is on the 8th cusp becoming the significator of death. Jupiter, the ruler of the house of death, is in the 5th opposing Mars and Uranus, to signify his undoing. Venus also is in the 8th house and shares with Jupiter in signifying the circumstances of dissolution. Alexander feasted and debauched for six days (Jupiter in the 5th), and was finally poisoned (Venus in the

8th) and died a great distance from home (Sagittarius on the cusp of the 8th).

From these indications and others it is possible to conclude that if Julian was not the reincarnation of Alexander he was certainly the incarnation of a person much like Alexander in many respects—a brilliant military genius whose ambitions were inordinate and against the balancing and reasoning forces of Jupiter.

It is also interesting to ask the fate of the soul of Julian after it was freed from the body of the Roman Emperor. Move the horoscope so that the 2nd house becomes the Ascendant and try to solve the mystery of the next life of Julian the Apostate.

ASTROLOGY AND KARMA

HOW WE MAKE OUR OWN FATE

THERE is no fatal necessity in the stars," wrote Lord Bacon, "and this, more prudent astrologers have consistently allowed."

Opponents of astrology frequently advance the argument that belief in the influence of the heavenly bodies leads to a fatalistic attitude towards all the problems of life. We all like to think of ourselves as free agents. We chafe at any factor of restraint, physical or psychological. We all like to talk about free countries, free speech and free trade. The very thought of freedom has bcome a fetish. We rise in righteous wrath against anyone who seeks to curb the spontaenous abandon of our actions. We acknowledge no authority superior to our own desires, and feel that the democratic theory of government has released us forever from supervision and restraint. Are we not all born free and equal? May not the humblest child hope to be a Senator when he grows up? Were not all our great capitalists, prize-fighters and movie stars once humble and insignificant persons? Every man knows he is the equal of every other man and superior to most. Success is a matter of "breaks." Even the subtle restraint of the merit system, demanding certain standards of thought and action, has been dissipated by the equality complex.

The materialist views astrology as a sort of astral theology. He feels that old orthodoxies are being fed to him again under a new name. He feels the influence of the heavenly bodies to be as improbable as heaven and hell, and relegates angels and planets to a common limbo. The modern man, wise with the conceits of twentieth century scholasticism, can find nothing in the universe nobler than himself, and settles down to a fanatical veneration of his own superiority.

It is not of course within the province of any science to convert a man against his will, yet even a little thought must convince the reasonable-minded man that some principle of order binds together the far flung purposes of the cosmos. It certainly cannot be scientifically demonstrated that the universe is merely one vast accident manifesting by means of innumerable lesser accidents. Despite the conceits of mortals, the vast pageantry of cosmic order manifests throughout its every part absolute and immutable law.

The very thought of this cosmic law oppresses and disturbs the lawless mortals of this generation. Man hates to think that he is a mere atom moved by inevitable and immutable laws. Egotism is the most easily offended of the conceits, and man is mortally offended by the immensities of the universe about him.

The universe of the wise man is unendurable to the foolish. To ease the aching of his personal pride, the Sophist has decreed that space be regarded as mindless and soulless, that man alone is endowed with sovereign reason, decreed by the accident of fate to become master of all the works of the Infinite Will.

How different from this modern attitude was the gentler vision of the ancients. They held all creation to be ensouled by a divine will and a universal purpose. Instead of being offended by the sense of their own smallness, they rejoiced in the vastness and sufficiency of the wisdom that preserved all life and sustained the order of cosmic progress.

It was among the wisest of ancient nations that philosophy and astrology grew up together, each accepted as a complement of the other. Nor was antiquity enfeebled by a sense of fatalism. Rather, it rejoiced in the recognition of immutable institutions of law in which no elements of change or accident existed. Having discovered and accepted the great laws of life, the philosophers of antiquity put their own lives in order, gladly acknowledging the sovereign wisdom which regulated justly and certainly all celestial and terrestrial affairs.

The law of Cause and Effect is one of the most important of the seven great laws by which, according to the ancient wisdom, the universe is sustained. The acceptance of this law and the understanding of its inferences is found in nearly all of the old systems of religion and science. Over forty great nations of the past have preserved this law in their scriptures by the statement which we call the Golden Rule. Unrecognized by most, this same law preserves all the consistencies of life and action.

The farmer plants his seed with perfect assurance that it will grow. Science accepts this law in every laboratory experiment. We live from day to day sustained by the conviction that certain causes will always produce consistent effects, and we have never yet been disappointed.

Yet very few people apply the law of Cause and Effect to personal action, sometimes because of ignorance, but more often, as already observed, because the training of the modern man has caused him to feel that he is in some way superior to or apart from the ordinary edicts of nature.

The great philosopher of India, Gautama Buddha, once said: "Effect follows cause as the wheel of the cart follows the foot of the oxen." We live in a world completely ruled by a law of universal compensation. Most of the miseries which now afflict this suffering mortal kind are due to our ignoring the principle of compensation in action. We do not sense the profound moral inference behind the story of the sowing and the reaping.

It is perfectly natural to ask how does astrology fit into this picture. What part do the stars play in the administration of the law of Cause and Effect? To understand this point we must also have recourse to another law of the ancients—Reincarnation. Life is eternally building, constantly improving vehicles for its own expression.

For our present purpose we narrow this subject down to the life of man, for as Socrates once wisely observed, "The proper study for mankind is man."

Reincarnation applied to man teaches that each human being has already lived many times upon this earth and in future ages will frequently return. The present life of a person is therefore not the whole of his existence, but a mere fragment.

Causes leading up to this present existence are not always evident in this life, nor are the consequences, which, arising from present action, will manifest in some future life. The ancients believed that from the horoscope it was possible to discover certain generalities of the previous life.

The law of Cause and Effect, when applied particularly to human concerns, was called by the ancients Karma. Karma does not mean fatalism, but rather, compensation. When a man buys something on credit he creates a debt, and the law declares that he must pay that debt. In a material, economic transaction this would not be regarded as fatalism, but as responsibility. Every action which a human being performs may thus be regarded as a cause, and every cause thus set in motion must have an effect consistent with itself. This is not fatality, this is compensation, or Karma.

In this unphilosophic age we all like to hope that by some mysterious formula we can escape the responsibilities of destructive action. We want to be selfish, but we do not want to suffer the reactions of selfishness. We constantly break natural law and we are all seeking some panacea which will remove from us the unhappy consequences of our indiscretions. The theological doctrine of the forgiveness of sin is a salve to take the sting from the reactions of iniquity, but the law of Cause and Effect can never be evaded, and all the evils that we do return to us again. There is no escape from any part of them.

The law of compensation, or Karma, has two distinct aspects. Good Karma is the beneficent reaction of constructive action. Fine and noble causations produce like consequences, bringing us joy and security and the good things of life. Bad Karma is the reaction of destructive action. Evil causes set in motion produce evil consequences, resulting in the miseries and misfortunes which afflict this present life.

When we are born into this world there are three factors working together, molding and modifying our existence here. The first is good Karma, which brings certain privileges of happiness and improvement and surrounds us with such good things as we have earned. The second is bad Karma, which manifests as the difficulties of the hour and the apparent evil fatality which dogs our footsteps. The third factor is action itself, our individual expression which is constantly making new Karma, good or bad according to the merit of the action itself.

Philosophy therefore teaches us to be modest in success (good Karma), patient in adversity (bad Karma), and constructive in all action. A life so lived promises future lives of greater enlightenment and happiness.

The law of Cause and Effect controls among other things the actual phenomenon of birth itself. We are born at the time which we have merited, and into conditions which we have merited, and into opportunities suitable for the next stage of our development. Each person is in the place he has earned for himself, and if he is dissatisfied with his present condition then he must set up within himself the causes which will result in a better state.

Astrology is the mechanism which administers the law of Karma. The universe is vibration. The interaction of the heavenly bodies is constantly setting up fields of specialized vibration. The incarnating entity of man is also a rate of vibration, modified by the Karmic factors within itself. The incarnation of the individual is determined by these vibratory factors. He is born into circumstances consistent with the Karmic modifications of his own nature. He is born when the planets are arranged in a pattern consistent with his own Karma. With his first breath, man breathes in the sidereal influences; and what he has merited comes to him from the stars and becomes the individuality determinant for his entire life.

The stars then are not merely sending baneful influences upon some poor weak, helpless mortal. They are really administering universal justice, bestowing upon each according to his own works. This is not fatalism. It is compensation. One of the first things that every philosopher must learn is to pay gladly the debts which he has incurred in nature. All Karma, both good and bad, leads finally to enlightenment through experience.

It is very often possible to determine to some degree the Karmic elements in life from the horoscope, for in many respects the nativity is a statement of indebtedness, a bill rendered to each of us when we are born. In it are set forth the debits and credits of Karma, as these apply directly to the present life.

The path of progress is with the Sun, and as Karma arises from past action it is most apt to be revealed through the qualities of the signs preceding those occupied by the Sun and the Ascendant in this present life.

As you realize, the signs of the zodiac are alternately positive and negative. The positive signs are Aries, Gemini, Leo, Libra, Sagittarius and Aquarius. The negative signs are Taurus, Cancer, Virgo, Scorpio, Capricorn and Pisces. To understand what is meant by positive and negative, it would probably be more appropriate to use the terms objective and subjective. Objective signs gain experience by contact with external sources of knowledge and objectify impulses. The subjective signs are much more introverted and their reactions rise from within themselves rather than from external contact. The positive and negative signs alternating represent an ebb and flow of energy. The Oriental philosophers symbolized it by an inbreathing and outbreathing an alternating process of externalizing. These signs themselves are closely related therefore to Cause and Effect, the positive signs being causes, and the negative signs effects or actions and reactions.

Persons born under the positive signs of the zodiac are not so apt to sense the Karmic factors in life as those born under the more sensitive psychical negative signs. This does not mean that the positive signs escape cosmic law, but they interpret impulses so definitely into action that they seldom feel the retributive aspect of energy. This explains why people born under the negative signs are much more fatalistic than their positive sign brothers and sisters.

You may have already observed that each of the zodiacal signs includes among their key-word qualities belonging to previous signs. I believe that each sign works out the Karma of the previous sign. Also, each sign rebels against the limitations of the previous sign. The sign of the zodiac under which we are born reveals not only the personal tendencies of the present personality but also brings forward a statement of unfinished business from the past. If previous action has merited a fortunate Karma, then the qualities of the sign are positively stated. If previous action merits an unfortunate Karma, then the negative responds to the negative vibration of the sign. All of the sideral influences are in themselves neutral, but they manifest as constructive or destructive according to the merit of the individual himself.

Let us consider the signs in their order, bearing in mind especially the workings of the law of Karma:

Aries, the first sign, is in itself positive, but it carries with it much of the negativeness of Pisces, the preceding sign. There is no more certain indication of weakness than constant effort to be strong, or an over-statement of ambition. Aries is a sign of rebellion against the limitations and restraint of Pisces. Disappointment may be considered an Aries characteristic. Persons born under the sign are constantly struggling to overcome obstacles, not realizing that their greatest obstacle is the Piscean weakness within themselves.

Taurus is a negative sign, but persons born under it are in many ways more positive than negative in their impulses. Many men successful in industry and the military are born under this supposedly negative sign. The reason is, the inordinate ambitions of Aries lie in the Karmic background of all Taurus people. The reason the sign is termed negative is because very often these dynamic impulses are blocked in their manifestation by the inflexible Taurean temperament. Ambition is locked in and comes to nothing, unless the Taurean person subjects his life to a powerful self-discipline. Even the successful Taurean people are notoriously unhappy. Whatever they achieve is unsatisfying, and they live and die

(41)

in bondage to unfulfilled desires. Their Aries Karma denies them contentment.

Gemini is considered to be a strong, positive intellectual sign, but throughout all of its aspects it is dominated by the subjective emotional impulses of Taurus. Gemini people are notoriously irritable and inconstant. One of the chief professions of the sign is writing, and literature as a whole is emotional and artistic, and its inspiration comes much more from Venus than from Mercury. Mercurial people are strongly temperamental, often moody, and not infrequently have morbid imaginations. The negative Mercurial frequently lacks integrity and is largely dominated by impulses and sense gratification, which is brought over from Venus the ruler of Taurus.

Cancer is a negative sign, strongly sympathetic and frequently a victim of inadequate mental control. The bad Karma of Gemini works out through the dubious reasoning powers of the Cancer type. The undeveloped Cancer persons develop the most extraordinary attitudes on the numerous problems of life and relationships. Their sympathies do their thinking for them and sentimental antipathies breed furious dislikes. Failure to orient in the intellectual sphere while living under the

Gemini influence means a scattered existence under Cancer, with the thinking powers partly eclipsed by the hallucinations of the sentiments.

Leo is a positive sign, but is frequently a victim of the evils of the sign Cancer. Unbalanced Leo types frequently suffer from some form of obsession, a malady peculiar to the psychism of Cancer. The obsession may range from a divinity complex to a highly aggravated infallibility complex. Leo people frequently feel that they are not as other mortals, that they are made by a special pattern, peculiarly endowed with semi-divine attributes. Their professions may vary, but whether they be evangelists or dictators, artists or financiers, they are overwhelmed with the impulse to reform. Cancer is a sign of parenthood and teaching and Leo people feel that they are the fathers and teachers of all mankind.

Virgo is a negative sign and is, so to speak, the let-down from Leo. Virgo people very often find Leo circumstances thrust upon them and they are forced by conditions beyond their control into positions of responsibility and leadership. The Virgo mind naturally seeks comfort, security and protection, but is seldom privileged to enjoy either. It is a sign of responsibility and signifies the servant and the bread-winner. The sign of Leo is frequently associated with monetary affairs and the problems of Virgo are usually monetary ones. If Virgo inherits a good Karma from its Leo past, then it may be placed in positions of responsibility and trust and become an administrator of power and authority. If the Leo person has trampled on others in his path to power, he is apt to find his Virgo incarnation one of hopeless limitation and financial reverse.

Libra is a positive sign and is regarded as one of the most artistic of the twelve. Though under the rulership of Venus, Libra manifests many tendencies of the Mercurial sign which precedes it. Libra frequently revolts against class limitation and rises to superiority usually from humble ancestry. In other words, it is a climbing sign. Two good examples of this climbing tendency of Libra are Napoleon Bonaparte and Adolph Hitler. Virgo symbolizes the proletariat and the fundamental psychology of Libra is a struggle against mediocrity. From its Virgo background the Libra type also secures the capacity to judge human nature. Libra types become public idols because of the ability to handle people. Their bad Karma however frequently limits their capacity to remain in high position, and disaster follows honor.

Scorpio is a negative sign, yet in many ways it manifests a strength not always to be found in positive signs. But again the course of the impulses is introverted. Scorpio's great problem is emotional control. The emotions of Scorpio are derived from Mars, the ruler of the sign, but from the accumulated Karma of Libra ruled by the emotional planet Venus. Libra signifies justice and its symbol is the scales. But where bad Karma has caused the Libra native to depart from standards of integrity, the distortion of the justice sense comes out in Scorpio, where truth becomes involved in a thousand emotional reflexes and loses all semblance to integrity. It is the bad Karma of Scorpio to always know that it is right whether it is right or not. It becomes its own standard of integrity. In a highly advanced Scorpio this sense of justice may be highly perfected and lead to great attainment in the occult arts, but in a less developed type judgment is usually hopelessly biased by the intensities of the emotions.

Sagittarius is a positive sign and seems to deliberately revolt againt the introversions of Scorpio. The Sagittarian is a good organizer and promoter. He receives these qualities as a legacy from Scorpio, but he puts them to much more evident use. The Sagittarian is usually entirely open and above-board with his plans. This is a reaction from the Scorpio secretiveness. Sagittarius is a religious sign which again is due to the strong emotional influence of Scorpio. Sagittarius is also the sign of long journeys on water, yet is not itself a water sign but borrows its affinity to liquids from Scorpio. Sagittarians frequently engage in occupations of a Scorpio nature, as medicine, occultism, diplomacy, etc. The Karmic tie between the two signs often manifests as dissipation which is a negative Scorpio weakness.

Capricorn is a negative sign, though in many ways one of the strongest and most enduring of the twelve. In no sign is there more danger of introversion than in this one. The negative quality of the sign turns all the impulses back upon themselves and makes normal mental, emotional and physical expression difficult. Yet Capricorn people are filled with the bubbling enthusiasm of Sagittarius. They are an independent, ambitious, naturally progressive group of people, but their normal expression is made almost impossible because of a peculiar crystallized personality. The Capricorn person inherits from his Sagittarian in-

carnation high aspirations and widely scattered resources. The lesson of Capricorn is a
moderating of all extremes of living. Most
of all, the Capricorn native must master the
impatience and inordinate ambition of the
Sagittarian and settle down to an apprecia-
tion of reasonable and simple things. Capricorn people are often unhappy not so much
from the evils of their state, but from the com-
parison between their present position and
some abstract standard towards which their
ambitions are pointed.

Aquarius is the last of the positive signs and
inherits from Capricorn a peculiar fixation of
viewpoint in the midst of an otherwise almost
complete inconsistency. Aquarius is termed
the sign of the liberals, and from social reform to dietetics the Aquarian is apt to be
found pointing out the advantages of something new and the hopeless disadvantage of
things as they are. It may be said that Aquarians are born in the objective case. One that
I know once referred to himself as one of
the cranks that make the world go round.
The sign is original and capable, and receives
from Capricorn certain psychic undercurrents
which strongly influence all of its activities.
First it embodies the Capricorn tenacity of
viewpoint and at the same time it lives in a

constant state of revolt against Capricorn conservatism and accepted institutions. From Capricorn also comes a definite strain of melancholia, and like Capricornians, Aquarians have very few close friends. This is not because people do not like them but because they cannot penetrate the Aquarian aura of super-individuality. The Aquarians should try to overcome the Capricorn Karma of isolation and try to mingle in a happy genuine way with the numerous interests of mankind.

Pisces is the last sign of the Zodiac and is also a negative sign. As the 12th house rules Karma particularly and Pisces is the 12th house sign and the last division of the Zodiac, it has special Karmic significance. Aquarius is the greatest energy waster in the Zodiac, because people born under that sign do not know how to relax. This waste is reflected in the debilities of the Piscean. Pisces also is completing a cycle and gathering up the loose ends of incarnations in the preceding eleven signs. The result is a heavy load of Karma. When the Karmic debt to the universe has been paid in the Pisces incarnation, the incarnating soul is then ready to start out afresh with a considerable part of Karma sublimated into soul power.

CPSIA information can be obtained
at www.ICGtesting.com
Printed in the USA
LVHW101544310123
738309LV00006B/402